the stone chair in an empty picnic field

(collected images & poetry by Caroline Julia Moore)

~ published by Artesian Thought ~

Copyright © 2012, Caroline Julia Moore

All rights reserved. No part of this publication may be reproduced, distributed, or transmitted in any form or by any means, or stored in a database or retrieval system, without the prior written permission of the author.

Published by Artesian Thought:
www.artesianthought.com

ISBN-10: 061568713X
ISBN-13: 978-0615687131 (Artesian Thought)

Artwork by Caroline Julia Moore.
Book Design & Editing by Artesian Thought.
First Edition: October, Two Thousand Twelve

Dedication

This book is dedicated to Kirk Alexanda Wright in recognition of his incredible bravery and strength in the face of adversity.

Table Of Contents

Plate I : 10
Little Poem of Hope : 11
Plate II : 12
The Eldest Angel : 13
Plate III : 14
Little Poem of You : 15
Plate IV : 16
In The Morning Light : 17
Plate V : 18
KiKi Soars : 19
Plate VI : 20
Little Poem of Stars : 21
Plate VII : 22
Resolution : 23
Plate VIII : 24
The Night Before A Miscarriage : 25
Plate IX : 26
Masks : 27
Plate X : 30
Chasms of Indigo : 31
Plate XII : 32

Notes of Japanese Cherry Blossom :...33
Plate XIII :..34
Cotard's Desertion :..35
Plate XIV :...36
The Lighthouse :..37
Plate XV :...38
Dystonia :..39
Plate XVI :... 40
Home Run :.. 41

Little Poem of Hope

Stand still: reflection beats down on us un-oppressed
Like the drum of a one two three four five six heart.
Relentless in a symphony where threads emerge
Entwined. We are unaware, naive and uncaring.

A night in September draws in around our screens,
The flicker, flicker light of a button switching on.
Let us not repeat our failings. Let us rise
Up onto the luscious verge of no restriction
Where we are unabated by bitterness, just simply being
Alive where we breathe. Seeing what we see and
Hearing the poignancy of a gut wrenching song.
Within a rush of something relentless don't stop
Don't stop, don't stop.

The Eldest Angel

I have no words that are sufficient for you
Who was abandoned by the one you curled within.
The arms you crawled inside to feel safe.

But the wisdom you gave me surpasses
The hard tainted sphere that is my grief.
I am so sorry that I let you down.
But within your power lies your enlightenment.

Your joy and creativity
Waits to drop like Autumn leaves
Inside a Season of burnished colours.
There is a golden heat contained in your hands.
Be a brave adventurer.
All random thoughts will be glorious stories
For your life to wrap itself within.

Little Poem of You

You wonder which colours will reach out like voices.
Emotion transcending media like a synaesthesiac.
I am sound, I am colour, I am a sad siren of 'missing you's.
The icey coldness in separation. Words washing
In cool circles of beads that curl around my wrist.
Up, out and through the door on the other side
Of the falling rain.
And I swear I see you smiling at me
From a shiny wet sphere.

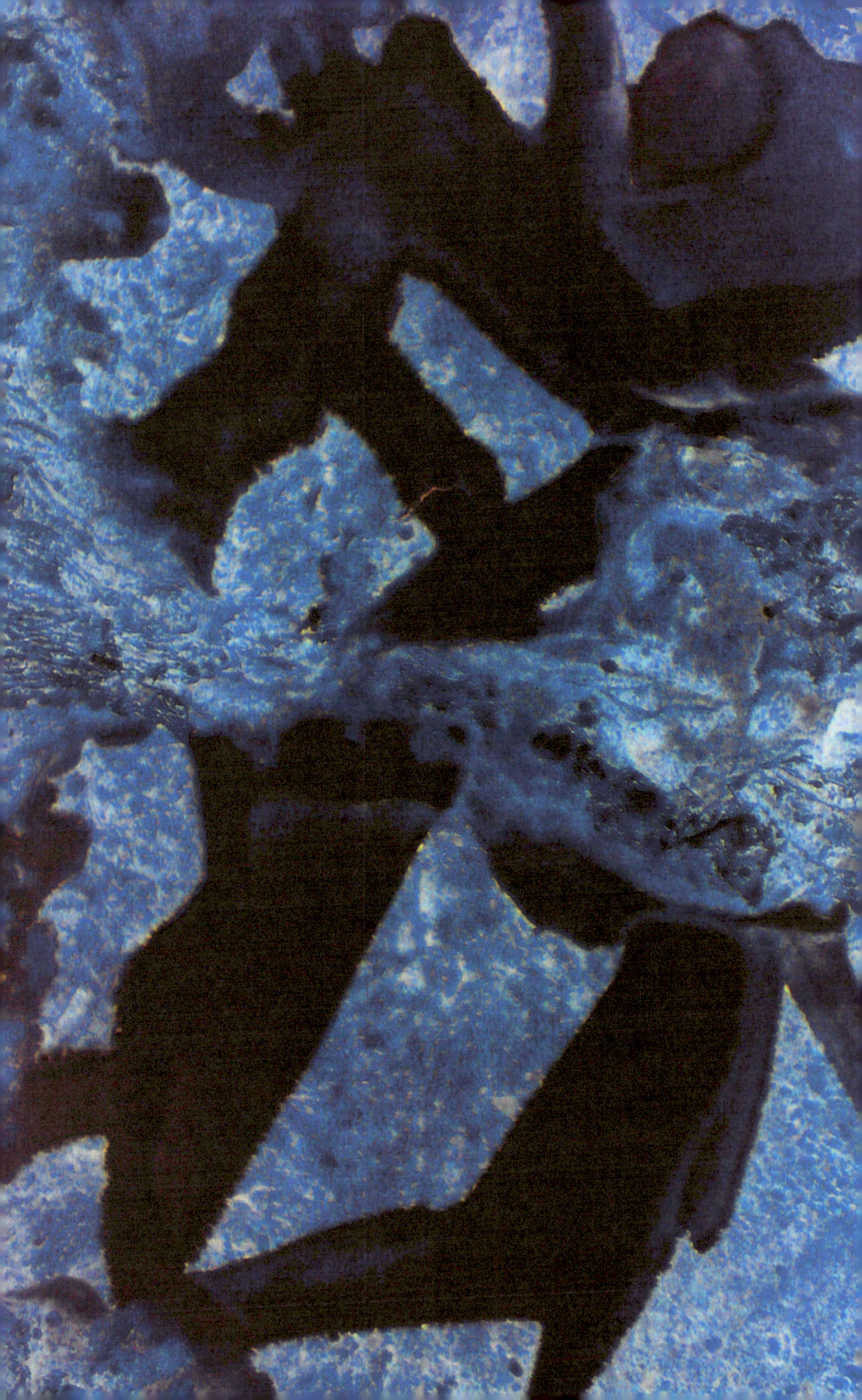

In The Morning Light

As the night surrounded me I dreamt of you
In stone green and bee stung mouth.
Framed in a arc of completeness.
You were there in the soft light of dusk
Like a image of a snow storm I could
Not quite touch.

Melting like fractals of ice on my hand;
A beautiful tenderness of presence.
As perfect as the precision of mathematics.
And I could not breathe, I could not move,
I could not get the words to speak.
Every sinew in locked awe of someone who
Caught me.

But daytime air infiltrated my song
And consumed me whilst the blizzard loaded your door.
And in everything you felt and everything you promised
It was always about her.
And I am left staring out as the snow falls.

KiKi Soars

The notice board of children's memories fell from the wall;
Laid bare on the step of possibilities.
Their imaginations still stabled with handprints and colouring.
Not wanting to hang on; every time I try it falls again.

In the echo of this sound I learn something devastating.
Night-time car crash and you were just gone.
Something broke in me and I struggle to explain.

You challenged the cold of our technology;
A flower switched to ultraviolet.
You were something like the sea.
Beautifully relentless.

Little Poem of Stars

The sun shines down on me and I become a gold thing
Within the glow of my contentedness.
You are like the star that is one of me
And all of me and none of me at the same time.

In the night's black sky we rain down together
And touch against each other gently as we fall.
Soft wonderment catches us as we glimpse a future
That brightens our smiles and shows in our eyes.
Together we fall, together we fall.
Our thoughts the colours of our rainbow containment.

Resolution

Screaming in an echo; let me out, let me out, let me
Grasp the risks that bleed right through me.
Just to unlock something outward and stop it
Crowding in and moving close into a still and dark lake.
The pools of calmness unnerve me so,
The drowning children sunken and softly calling.

Tiny Christening bracelets shimmering in their silver
And clinging to wasted and skeletal fragile wrists.
Oh so very, very small and brittle; a home
For stinging dragonfly eggs.
Inside a bed of sludgy moss reside the fingernails
Of striving and clawing; released with so much longing,
Sharp scratches on the cheekbones
Of symmetrical beauty and we so want to be her.

Just melt into the perfection that is our
Tangled and twisted and awe stricken deformity.
For one day our terrified angels will embrace us
In a holding that is very much complete.
Everything we laughed at will overwhelm us in
Its entirety, for we are lulled in our auras
That glisten on water reeds.

And the birth of everything we repressed
Will be subtle and within us; so very still.
Nothing will rot us more than we are torn
And this brings us to smile as the quiet beneath is
Astounding.

The Night Before A Miscarriage

Cat napping in the afternoon with my two babies.
One curled up in my arms, a content little Buddha.
The other spinning within me like an invisible spaceman
Hanging from the silk of desire for life.
A heart beat crawling in an arid desert whilst her brother
Whimpers in his sleep.

There is a smug curve to my mouth, unknowingly
Engraving my babies in my memory.
A joyous togetherness of mother, son and daughter.
No lambs to the slaughter, we will be strong.
These thoughts settle a strange panic within me
As my eyes close and bring me to calm sleep.

Outside of the window there is a bright light
Raining into nothing.

Masks

How do we run? Backwards, forwards, sideways; no,
No just away, as far as we can into the deepest and emptiest
Room that swamps us in the safety of unfeeling.

Down, down and down again inside our life force that is
Un-reliant on anyone else.
But does that help us?
Do we hide to preserve our Amazonian bravado?
All these question marks just irritate when surely we can
Survive within our own stage, our platform of 'who gives a fuck?'

And look at how strong and resilient we are.
The only smears of lipstick across my face are caused
By a hand irritated by the mask of my own okay-ness;
The outward shield of dishevelment as a banshee
Laughs and cries at oh-so-carefully measured psychosis.

Those who fear our insanity are the ones who destroyed
Our faith, our purity, our longing and stupidity in trusting.
Who long for sense and rhythm in our writing when there is none;
When they were the ones who destroyed our ability to see the
Still beauty within the curve of a sea shell.

White Noise

In the afternoon I watched a crow fly knowingly
Into the cold garage door.
Twitching with still gaze and wired determination.

Black arrow fighter plane.

In the war zone of dull light
He sat down in the big stone chair of an empty picnic field.
Took a gun to his head; fingers clawed and shaking.

The sentence choked with too many words
Never quite found the way out.
A throat swollen with the stinging nettles
He forgot to fold over.

This sphere contains volcanic ash.

Chasms of Indigo

I so very much want to hear your voice.
To close my eyes and see the deepest ever indigo
Melting over my inability to sleep, my sharp stop of
Inspiration. Paint me with your prosody, just let me be
Lost.
And hold me slowly as I ask you to fold yourself
Within me. I no longer dream of jumping forward
In queues at the bank; up to the best seat in the house,
That is never what was meant for me. To be first,
I laugh, this is the greatest joke with an irony
Only I can see. I never was that girl with the brightest
Most beautiful radiating smile.
Like the butterfly who evolved to be the smudgy, ordinary
Grey brown of the industrial revolution, my evolution
Pulls me down to be insubstantial. The one that all
Settle for when their bright scarlet light has died.
And every single breath of my lovers longs to be else where.
Where the brightness of my purity only shines when
They have left. The bitter revenge has no Sweetness
When it is fuelled with such empty sorrow.
For all I ever gained was nothing, like the song that cries
Running to stand still. And I lie in my company trying to
Convince myself that I have everything I need but everything
I bleed will never release this void of never ever being
Good enough. See how awkward that is?
Stupidly each of them cry afterwards please come back,
Please come back, I knew not what I was losing.
Though oh, for your choosing, you are the dumbest in your
Throw away and discard. With every longing for me resonates
A thousand get out of my sights. And with each of those
This tiny fragile light just gets
Dimmer. Into the blue, the deepest darkest blue.

Notes of Japanese Cherry Blossom

And so the flower unfolds;
Note by note it gathers to life.
The tears he cried on the night I left
Rebuild the petals one by one.
His room fills with light;
Slow notes of Japanese cherry blossom.

He looks in my eyes from another bedroom.
The hands on my clock edge forward,
And I smile for I am the seconds and
The firefly drawn to it's moving hands,
As into my room his presence floods.

I walk with him fast and entwining my fingers
I feel calm warmth from his hand on mine.
The green of his eyes throws me in soft water
And every thought echoes reassurance as
The time edges on to a shared midnight.

He enthrals me. Bewitched and consumed
My heart in my throat a thudding time bomb
As his footsteps carry him nearer.
He catches my smile full of fireflies, released
From the scent of Japanese cherry blossom.

Cotard's Desertion

He should have died when he was seven;
Instead the now is a forced, violet dissociated life.
Godforsaken wakefulness unabated by endless pills;
Those tiny circles of promises never fulfilled.

If only he could sleep; to feel like he had woken up.

In the morning, a seed in denial of existence
Was planted to cling like Lorenzo's leaves of basil.
Energy and light severed by brutality.

He falls away from the ground control of a bed
Belonging to a recuperated child revisiting who he was.
Left in limbo, a ghost in his machine;
Vapour from a kettle; going, going
Not quite gone.

The Lighthouse

To the lighthouse our broken souls run.
In climbing it's stairs our minds are spinning,
But the whirring reassurance of brittle orange light
Is what draws us upwards.

I am out of breath so you stop to enfold me,
The warmth of you makes me so resolute.
We lead all our achings for yesterday
And dispel them into shards of light,
Throwing out the way into a new future.

Let us spill out the pain of our torn, tangled hearts
To guide boats away from the jagged rocks
And find a smile within the reflection
Of a beacon on the sea.

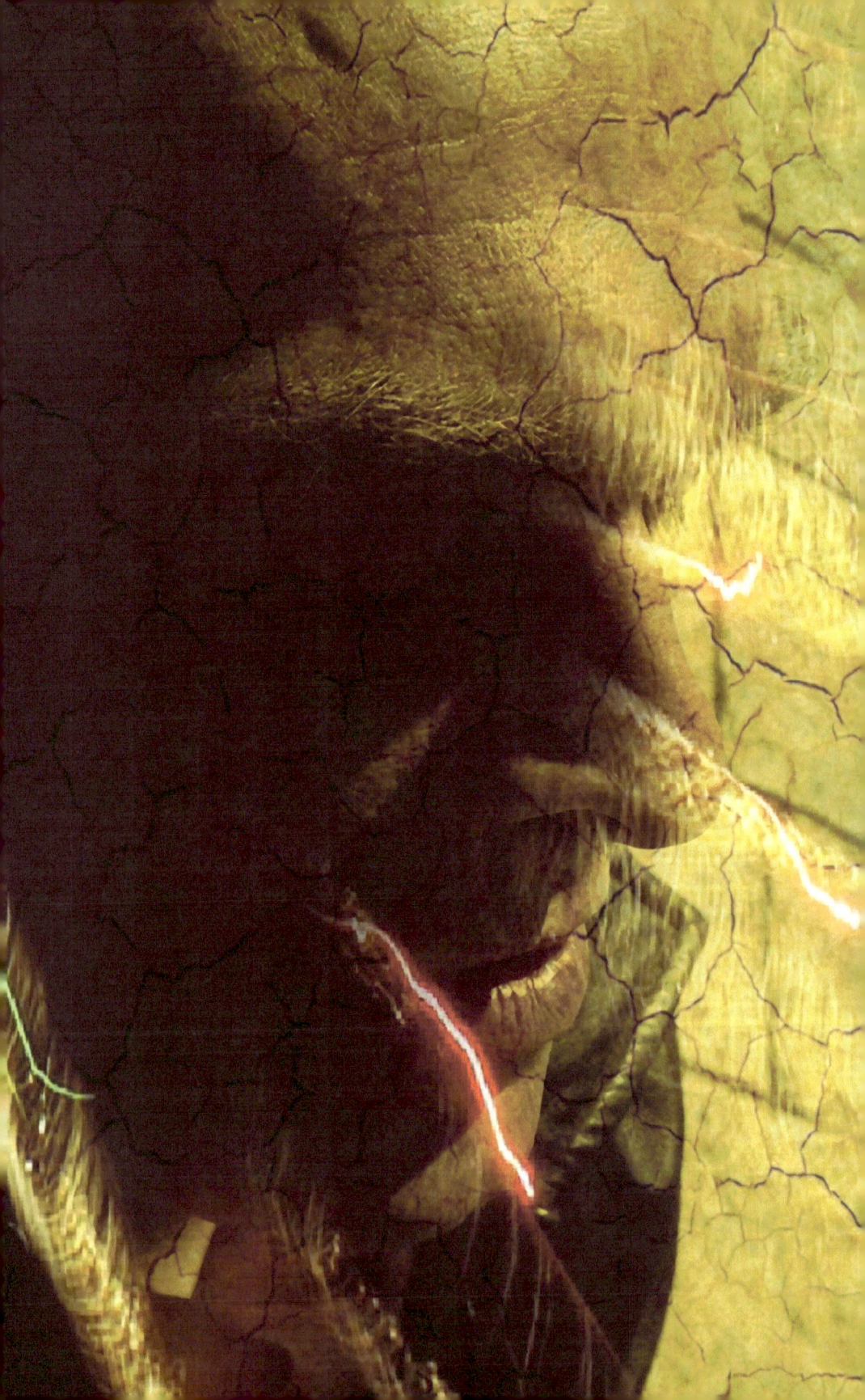

Dystonia

Wrapped up in my skull of slow grenade I heard you
Downstairs, calling to me. A voice so real.
Within the ribcage of my existence my heart hit hard.
Like tumbleweed abandoned you moved on silent air
And a blackened cord stifled your fight for breath.
Against a bloodened battlefield you mocked their distain;
Laughing in their faces.
Photograph of a child running out across the sand
Unknowing the quickness of the pull under.

I found an ammonite on the shingle that had hidden
From the tourist.
Within my fingers it turned and left a burst of words.
And I understood like I understand
The petrified awe of entrapment.
The stillness and control that I hold in my hand
Ripped from your adolescence,
Where everything you wished for will be quiet still.
Me by a dark shore, as the evening draws in; staring out.
The sea at night was breathing in its huge expanse
Within placid darkness on a calm breeze.

There was a malevolent spirit under thick blankets.

A gun shot fired on silent; shattering glass pain.
And I miss you, and I miss you, and I miss you.
Into our own separation we tumble.
Our sinews molten, twisting as the us is locked in.
Something waiting.
Opium seeds hidden in red.
My bones are metallic. I am a bird cage full of empty.
I am a slow grenade that longs to be detonated by your understanding.
Dystonic; forgive me, I know not what I do.

Home Run

We lie on shattered glass; our test and our price for adoring.
But we are not players of typed illusions and manipulated sighs.
We are the transcended on the flight of the ethereal;
The masters of our ability to feel alive
And to plead with no-one for our hands of giving.

We fall seven times to stand again for eight.
We fail nothing.
Every fragile tiny atom binds within the metaphysical cat that
Shows no illusions in our reality.
We rise above time.
We are above disappointment and so our numbness will protect
The parts of us we scored out once then over and over.
No-one but the brave will dare again to breathe.
And we are breathing.

Caroline Julia Moore

Caroline Julia Moore grew up in Kingston and moved to Camberwell, London to study for a psychology degree at Goldsmiths University in 1991. Her interest then focused on Neuropsychology and the study of language using functional imaging.

She won a prestigious scholarship award from The Brain Research Trust to research and write her PhD at The Institute of Neurology, Queens Square. She continued her research at The Institute of Psychiatry, London, where she investigated the effects of the genetic Fragile X Syndrome on brain anatomy and function.

In 2003 Caroline moved to Dorset, enthralled by its unique beauty, where she now lives with her three children. She continues to be inspired by the use of language and its ability to evoke imagery and emotion.

Her fascination with neuropsychological conditions influences both her artwork and her writing, with a particular awe of synaesthesia where senses become confused (such as hearing colours and seeing music). Caroline has been both the primary and co-author on a number of scientific publications. This is her first published collection of poetry and digital artwork.

www.ingramcontent.com/pod-product-compliance
Lightning Source LLC
Chambersburg PA
CBHW041756040426
42446CB00001B/48